T0407094

FUN AND GAMES

FIREWORKS

Multiplication

Jay Hwang

Consultants

Lisa Ellick, M.A.
Math Specialist
Norfolk Public Schools

Pamela Estrada, M.S.Ed.
Teacher
Westminster School District

Publishing Credits

Rachelle Cracchiolo, M.S.Ed., *Publisher*
Conni Medina, M.A.Ed., *Managing Editor*
Dona Herweck Rice, *Series Developer*
Emily R. Smith, M.A.Ed., *Series Developer*
Diana Kenney, M.A.Ed., NBCT, *Content Director*
Stacy Monsman, M.A., *Editor*
Kristy Stark, M.A.Ed., *Editor*
Kevin Panter, *Graphic Designer*

Image Credits: p.4 rkl_foto/Shutterstock.com; p.7 Art Phaneuf/Alamy Stock Photo; p.12 DD Images/Shutterstock.com; p.13 Matt Zambonin/Freestyle Photo/Getty Images); pp.14–15 aladin66; p.16 James.Pintar/Shutterstock.com; p.17 (front) Sergei Bachlakov/Shutterstock.com; p.17 (middle) Matt Zambonin/Freestyle Photo/Getty Images; p.17 (back) aladin66/iStock; pp.18–19 (back) aladin66/iStock; pp.20–21 Richard StonehouseWPA Pool/Getty Images; pp.20–21 (background) aladin66/iStock; pp.22–23 Marc Bruxelle/Alamy Stock Photo; p.24 (left) Matt Zambonin/Freestyle Photo/Getty Images; p.24 (right) Perry Mastrovito/Getty Images; p.25 Laurent Lucuix/Alamy Stock Photo.

Teacher Created Materials

5301 Oceanus Drive
Huntington Beach, CA 92649-1030
http://www.tcmpub.com

ISBN 978-1-4258-5806-3
© 2018 Teacher Created Materials, Inc.
Made in China
Nordica. 112017. CA21701237

Table of Contents

Boom! Bang! Bored?

Bang! Whoosh! Pop! Stella has a gigantic smile on her face as the glow from an orange burst erupts in the night sky. *Hiss! Snap!* The sound of a silver whistling whirl delights Stella's ears. *Boom!* Silence. *Bang!* A giant, blue flower explodes in the air. Stella cheers along with the crowd. Her father's fireworks sure are impressive. Behind the scenes, though, away from the crowd, Stella knows that her father is bored and unhappy.

Stella's father is a **pyrotechnician**. He sets off fireworks for a living, and it is his job to dazzle audiences with his firework show. But lately, Stella's father has become bored. He feels that he knows everything about fireworks. He can identify the exact **proportion** of ingredients needed to make any type of explosion. Barium is used for green fireworks and lithium for red fireworks. Shells loaded with many small, round pieces of metal called **stars** will create one large explosion. Adding more black powder to the **lift charge** at the bottom part of the firework will propel it higher into the sky, and changing the length of the **fuse** will **detonate** the firework at precisely the right time. To him, fireworks are simply careful calculations and measurements, which achieve a consistent, predictable result in color and sound. He feels that he has nothing left to learn.

Pyrotechnicians prepare for a firework show.

Professional pyrotechnicians plan for 2 hours to produce 1 minute of a firework show.

1. How many minutes of planning time is this?

2. How many minutes does it take to plan a 30 minute show?

A Bright Idea

Stella decides to help her father love fireworks again. She remembers a story he once told her. He was a young boy celebrating Independence Day with his family. He watched in amazement as a giant red star popped. He gasped as a white pinwheel fizzled. Those glittering explosions **inspired** him.

Suddenly, Stella has an idea. She remembers her father telling her about an event called the Fireworks Festival of Montréal. There, people compete to make the greatest firework displays in the world. Surely, this competition would help **reignite** her father's passion for fireworks.

A child celebrates while watching fireworks.

Chrysanthemum fireworks
light the sky over Montréal.

Montréal Festival website

Once the excitement wears off, Stella realizes she hasn't thought her plan through. How can she take her father to a festival in Canada? She doesn't have money for plane tickets, and she can't pay for a hotel. Stella realizes she has a new problem to solve.

Stella decides to search the festival's website for information. She quickly learns that the city of Montréal is holding a poetry contest to **promote** the festival. The winner will be awarded airfare, a hotel stay, and two free tickets to the festival.

"A poem about fireworks?" Stella wonders aloud. It will be challenging, but she is determined! For the rest of the night, Stella sits on her bed thinking about how fireworks make her feel.

Stella writes and revises. Finally, she's ready to submit. She takes a deep breath and presses the send button.

My Father's Fireworks

He sends round packages of light
into the night sky
where they burst at the seams
into dazzling arrays of colors,
which adults and children see
for miles and miles.
"My father's fireworks,"
I proudly exclaim,
"will bring happiness and joy
for many years to come!"

Weeks pass as Stella waits for the winner of the contest to be announced. Every day, she checks her email and mailbox for a response.

One day, an envelope arrives. The golden envelope with the stamp on it stands out in the stack of mail. Stella opens it and eagerly reads the card inside.

City Hall
275 Rue Notre-Dame Est
Montréal, QC H2Y 1C6

Miss Stella Garcia
1313 Mockingbird Lane
Mockingbird Heights, CA 90608

POSTES POSTAGE 25
CANADA

Montréal Fireworks Festival

Festival de l'International
des Feux Loto-Québec

La Ronde

ADMIT ONE

No refunds, exchanges or cancellation allowed

Bonjour, Stella!

    We absolutely love your poem about fireworks! We **cordially** extend an invitation to you and a guest to the International Montréal Fireworks Festival. Please join us for the best firework displays the world has to offer. The city of Montréal and our friendly **mascot** await your arrival!

Au revoir!

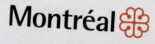

Montréal

Inside the envelope are two tickets to Montréal. She runs to her father and gives him the tickets. His eyes light up when he hears what Stella has done for him.

Then, with regret, her father says, "Unfortunately, I have too much work to do to go to Montréal. I want you and your mom to go and enjoy the festival. When you come back, you can tell me all about the fireworks."

Stella is disappointed but tells her father that she will do her best to enjoy the show.

Welcome to Montréal

Stella and her mom take a shuttle to the airport. They check their bags and wait for their flight.

The flight is pleasant as Stella gazes out the window at the small cities below. She wonders whether fireworks see the world in the same way. Before she knows it, the plane is landing in Montréal.

Visiting a new place is exciting, but Stella remembers that she has a mission. Stella and her mom look for the friendly mascot to meet them at baggage claim. It doesn't take long for them to see the bright orange mascot.

The furry creature approaches them and musically exclaims, "Stella! Fantastic! You're here!" The mayor of Montréal appears from behind the mascot.

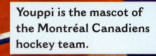

Youppi is the mascot of the Montréal Canadiens hockey team.

"On behalf of the city of Montréal, I am honored to welcome the Fireworks Festival's Poet, Stella!" announces the mayor. People in the airport cheer and clap for her. Stella's mom and the mayor shake hands.

The mascot chimes in, "My name is Youppi, but you can call me Yippee. I'll be your guide for the Fireworks Festival! Let's go to La Ronde!"

LET'S EXPLORE MATH

Montréal is about 4,588 kilometers away from Mockingbird Lane. Complete the area model to show how far Stella and her Mom will travel roundtrip.

$$4,588 \times 2 = _____$$

×	4,000	+ 500	+ 80	+ 8
2				

La Ronde

La Ronde is the second-largest amusement park in Canada. It has over 40 roller coasters, 2,400 vertical feet (732 vertical meters) of railway, and 20 restaurants. The Fireworks Festival is held inside La Ronde.

Stella and her mom are amazed at all the fun the amusement park has to offer. Yippee shows them around the entire park and goes on some of the rides with them. They share a lot of delicious foods, such as funnel cake and **poutine**.

Stella is having so much fun. Then, she sees a flyer for the Fireworks Festival and is quickly reminded of the reason she is there: the fireworks show! There is no time for clowning around. Her father is counting on her to tell him all about the amazing fireworks.

"Yippee, may we please go to the Fireworks Festival?" Stella asks.

"Of course!" shouts Yippee.

The group gets on a miniature train. Yippee tells the conductor to head straight for the Fireworks Festival preparation grounds. The conductor winks and tugs his hat. His small train takes off at its maximum speed of 2 miles per hour (3 kilometers per hour). Along the way, Stella, her mom, and Yippee make a few stops to take photos.

LET'S EXPLORE MATH

The small train at La Ronde travels about 3 kilometers per hour. One of the roller coasters has a maximum speed of 96 kilometers per hour. How many times as fast is the roller coaster than the small train?

Poutine is made of French fries, cheese curds, and gravy.

Meet the Competitors

The train chugs its way toward its next stop. Stella sees a group of people busily working. On their shirts, they have red leaves. The maple leaf is the emblem of Canada. Yippee announces to the Canadian team, "Our poet has arrived!"

The Canadian team members shake Stella's hand and warmly welcome her and her mom to the event. They tell Stella how much they love her poem. The team won the Fireworks Festival last year, and they received a standing **ovation** from the judges and the crowd.

Stella feels that the Canadian team members will have words to inspire her father. She asks, "What do fireworks mean to you?"

Stella's new friends think about the question. Then, they discuss their responses as a team. Finally, they agree upon an answer. The team leader responds, "Fireworks are the tools with which we express who we are as individuals, a team, a country, and as humankind."

Stella repeats his words to herself. She feels a deep connection to the team's answer. She thinks it will inspire her father. She will remember to tell him when she gets home.

Canadian team members

the Spanish team

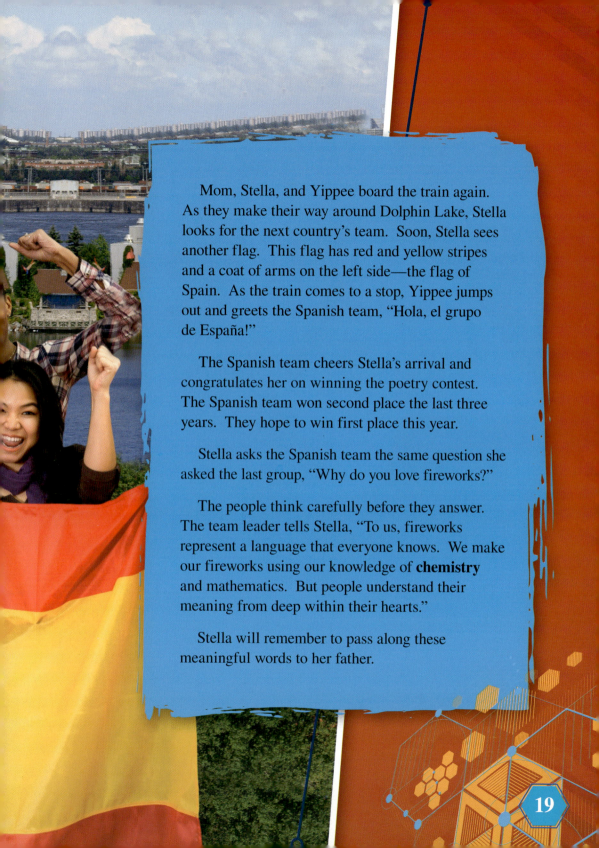

Mom, Stella, and Yippee board the train again. As they make their way around Dolphin Lake, Stella looks for the next country's team. Soon, Stella sees another flag. This flag has red and yellow stripes and a coat of arms on the left side—the flag of Spain. As the train comes to a stop, Yippee jumps out and greets the Spanish team, "Hola, el grupo de España!"

The Spanish team cheers Stella's arrival and congratulates her on winning the poetry contest. The Spanish team won second place the last three years. They hope to win first place this year.

Stella asks the Spanish team the same question she asked the last group, "Why do you love fireworks?"

The people think carefully before they answer. The team leader tells Stella, "To us, fireworks represent a language that everyone knows. We make our fireworks using our knowledge of **chemistry** and mathematics. But people understand their meaning from deep within their hearts."

Stella will remember to pass along these meaningful words to her father.

the Chinese team

"Time to get moving!" the conductor yells. Stella says good-bye to the Spanish team and wishes them luck.

The train quickly approaches the end of its tracks. Stella and her mom see another flag. This flag is red with yellow stars. The yellow stars remind Stella of fireworks. It is the flag of China.

The train comes to a stop. The Chinese team greets Stella, her mom, and Yippee. They tell Stella that fireworks are a big part of Chinese culture. Many historians believe that fireworks were invented there. China makes and sells more fireworks than any other country in the world.

LET'S EXPLORE MATH

Each country's team typically has 17 members. Suppose that 6 teams participate in the festival. How many team members are there altogether?

Stella asks them for their thoughts about fireworks. "What is the secret to making the best fireworks?"

The team members talk amongst themselves, and the eldest member answers Stella's question. "The secret to making the best fireworks is progress. Learn from those who know more than you, and teach those who know less than you. Fireworks have evolved from simple firecrackers to what they are now because of this progress."

Stella feels a sense of pride as she realizes that she is taking part in the **evolution** of future fireworks.

It's Showtime!

Back on the train, they make their way to the final stop. In about an hour, Stella will see the greatest fireworks display in the world. She feels a strong appreciation for all the hard work that goes into putting on the show. She can't wait to see what the Canadian team has planned. She looks forward to the artistry of the Spanish team's show. She hopes to learn from the techniques that the Chinese team will use.

She thinks about her father and how much work he puts into each of his firework displays. She hopes that her experience will soon give him the answers he needs to once again feel connected to his work.

The sun sets, and the sky darkens into a black canvas. The stage is set for the Fireworks Festival. Huge crowds begin to fill every part of La Ronde. People search high and low for places to view the fireworks. People in the city even settle on rooftops and in trees to see the show. Around the lake, teams run back and forth as they make final preparations.

Yippee guides Stella and her mom to their seats. Stella anxiously awaits the start of the show.

A ticket for a reserved seat at the festival costs about 54 Canadian dollars. Suppose that 36 people in a tour group want reserved seats. Use partial products to show how much their tickets cost altogether.

```
      5 4
    × 3 6
    ——————
      2 4    (___ × ___)
    —————    (  6 × 5 0)
             (3 0 ×   4)
  + 1,5 0 0  (___ × ___)
```

A crowd waits anxiously for the sky to darken so the fireworks show can begin.

Suddenly, music starts to fill the air at La Ronde. Tiny red flares flicker back and forth over the lake. Then, a **barrage** of white comets fan out like a tidal wave. A single shell is launched high into the sky before it bursts into a giant purple-and-red peony.

The music picks up speed. Before Stella knows it, whistling whirls, bees, and rainbow rosettes fly into the sky in a frenzy. Large flower shapes pulsate green to blue to red while willows fall like waterfalls in the sky below. The displays bring the sky to life as sound and color dance together in harmony. Stella lets out many *oohs* and *aahs*, and Yippee cries out "Yippee!"

Behind the scenes, all the teams look up in admiration. The long hours of hard work are finally paying off. Every measured ingredient, timed detonation, and thoughtful design is perfectly paying off. The night sky is filled with colorful fire, and the crowds appreciate the teams' hard work. The fireworks spread happiness and joy for miles and miles. As they watch, the teams already know that they can't wait to do it all again next year.

Red firework fountains spray light up from the ground.

Willow fireworks shower the Montréal sky.

LET'S EXPLORE MATH

Firework shows in other cities are not as huge as the Montréal festival. Suppose a city presents a 23-minute show. There are 152 firework effects each minute. How many effects are there in the show altogether?

The Grand Finale

After the last firework fades, Stella sits in a daze. It was beautiful. The judges tally their final scores for each of the competitors. Soon, the champion team will be named. In Stella's mind, every competitor deserves to be a world champion. She hopes that one day she will be as good at crafting and launching fireworks as they are.

Then, Stella remembers the final step of her important mission. She has to go home to tell her father about the firework show. She will also tell him about the inspirational, passionate, and wise words the teams shared with her.

Montréal International Fireworks Festival

Stella thinks that the fireworks would surely have inspired her father. If only he had been here to see them.

Just then, Yippee removes the head of his costume. Stella's jaw drops. Underneath the fuzzy orange costume is her father, grinning from ear to ear.

"I had no idea!" exclaims Stella as she turns to her mom.

"Dad wanted to surprise you, sweetie," says her mom.

"Thank you for reminding me about my love and passion for fireworks," Stella's father says as he gives Stella a big hug.

Fireworks come in many different sizes. So do firework shows. Shows run for varying lengths of time, and the number of firework shells that explode is related to the number of minutes. Imagine that you are a pyrotechnician for a firework company. Complete the table so that the other members of your team know the details of each type of show offered by the company.

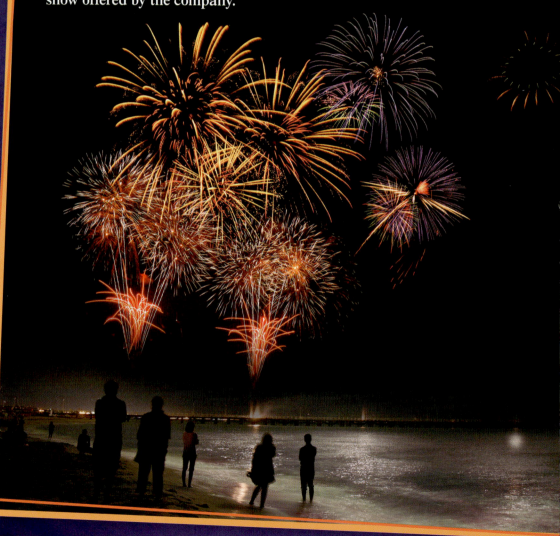

Fireworks Inc. | Safe & Spectacular

Firework Show Specifications

Show Size	Minutes	Shells per Minute	Total Shells
Mini			
Middle		200	2,200
	28	656	
Mega	30		
			36,000

Glossary

barrage—a large amount of something that comes quickly and continuously

chemistry—a type of science including the structure and properties of substances and the changes they go through

cordially—friendly and politely

detonate—to explode or to cause something to explode

evolution—a process of slow change and development

fuse—a string connected to an explosive device that is set on fire to cause the device to explode

inspired—caused or influenced someone to have an idea, or to create or do something

lift charge—black powder which is ignited to propel fireworks into the air

mascot—an object, animal, or person that represents a group or company and is used as a symbol, usually to bring good luck

ovation—moment in time when a group of people at a public event show enthusiastic approval or appreciation by clapping their hands

poutine—a Canadian dish of French fries topped with cheese curds and gravy

promote—to make people aware of an event through advertising

proportion—the relationship between the amount of two things

pyrotechnician—a person who has been trained to handle and use fireworks and is responsible for their safety and function

reignite—to give new life or energy to something or someone

stars—pellets that burn a certain color or make a certain spark effect

Index

Answer Key

Let's Explore Math

page 5:

1. 120 minutes

2. 3,600 minutes

page 13:

Area model shows product of 9,176 km; 4,588 × 2 = 8,000 + 1,000 + 160 + 16 = 9,176

page 14:

32 times as fast

page 21:

102 members

page 23:

Model shows product of 1,944 Canadian dollars; 6 × 4; 300; 120; 30 × 50

page 25:

3,496 firework effects

Problem Solving

11; 18,368; 1,200